Disclaimer:

The information provided in this book, "The Ultimate Guide to Getting Your House Ready for Sale", is for general informational purposes only. The author and publisher of this book have made every effort to ensure the accuracy of the information presented herein. However, the author and publisher do not guarantee or warrant the accuracy, completeness, or usefulness of any information contained in this book.

The information contained in this book is not intended to be a substitute for professional legal, financial, or real estate advice. Readers should always seek the advice of a licensed professional before making any financial or legal decisions related to the sale of their home.

The author and publisher of this book shall not be liable for any direct, indirect, incidental, consequential, or punitive damages arising from the use of, or reliance on, any information contained in this book. The author and publisher shall not be responsible for any errors or omissions in the information presented in this book.

The information presented in this book is subject to change without notice. The author and publisher of this book reserve the right to make changes to the information contained herein at any time, without prior notice.

The author and publisher of this book are not affiliated with any specific real estate company, financial institution, or contractor mentioned in this book. The inclusion of any specific company or service in this book is not an endorsement or recommendation of that company or service by the author or publisher.

By reading this book, you acknowledge and agree that you have read and understand this legal disclaimer. You further acknowledge and agree that the author and publisher of this book shall not be liable for any damages arising from your use or reliance on any information contained in this book.

About the Author:

Andy LaPointe is a seasoned professional with over 23 years of combined experience in the real estate and financial services industries. He began his career as a licensed Realtor, serving clients in residential and commercial real estate needs for eight years. After that, he transitioned into the financial services industry, working as a Series 7 stockbroker, Registered Investment Advisor (RIA), and mutual fund wholesaler for 15 years.

Throughout his career, Andy has shared his expertise with a wider audience. He has been invited to appear on several television news broadcasts on Channel 7 & 4 in Traverse City, where he discussed his tips, strategies, and techniques for selling a home. He has also been a featured guest on the popular Ron Jolly morning talk show on AM 580 - WTCM in Traverse City.

In addition to his media appearances, Andy has been featured in publications across the State of Michigan and beyond, including Crain's Detroit Business, Traverse City Business News, Cosmopolitan Home Magazine, and Traverse Magazine. Through his book, "The Ultimate Guide to Getting Your House Ready for Sale", he offers valuable insights and advice on preparing a home for sale.

As a real estate professional and financial expert, Andy understands how to guide individuals and families to design their ideal lifestyle and achieve their dreams. His experience and expertise make him a trusted advisor for those seeking to sell their homes and move on to their next adventure.

He is the author of two real estates books. The titles include:

Up North Dream: The Guide to Moving to Northern Michigan

Zoom Town USA: The Ultimate Guide to the Remote Work-Life Balance Lifestyle in a Modern-Rural Community

Table of Contents

Introduction:

Selling your home can be an emotional and overwhelming experience, especially when it is your first time navigating the intricate process. But, with the right knowledge and guidance, you can prepare your house for a successful and stress-free sale.

"Selling Made Simple: A Comprehensive Guide to Preparing Your House for Sale" is your go-to resource for understanding the ins and outs of preparing your home for the market. By following the strategies outlined in this book, you'll be well on your way to a profitable and rewarding home sale experience.

The importance of preparing your house for sale cannot be overstated. When potential buyers walk into your home, they're not just looking for a house; they're looking for a place where they can envision themselves living and creating new memories. To make your home stand out from the competition, you must ensure that it is in top-notch condition, showcases its best features, and appeals to a wide range of buyers. By doing so, you increase the likelihood of receiving multiple offers, which can ultimately lead to a higher selling price.

This book is designed to guide you through each step of the home-selling process, from assessing your home's condition and decluttering to staging, pricing, and navigating offers. Each chapter is filled with practical tips, expert advice, and real-life examples that will help you achieve the best possible outcome for your sale.

In Chapter 2, we'll dive into assessing your home's condition, identifying necessary repairs and updates, and prioritizing improvements for maximum impact. We'll also discuss the benefits of a pre-sale home inspection and how to consult with a professional to ensure your home is ready for the market.

Chapter 3 focuses on decluttering and organizing your home. We'll explore the psychology of decluttering and provide room-by-room strategies to help you eliminate clutter and maintain a tidy home throughout the showing process.

Next, in Chapter 4, we'll delve into the art of staging your home for success. You'll learn the importance of staging, the basics of furniture arrangement, lighting, and color schemes, and how to decide between DIY staging and hiring a professional stager.

Curb appeal is the first impression potential buyers have of your home, so in Chapter 5, we'll cover landscaping and lawn care, exterior maintenance and repairs, and ways to enhance your entryway to create a welcoming atmosphere.

Chapter 6 will provide you with a comprehensive guide to deep cleaning your home in preparation for showings. We'll share general cleaning tips and tricks, a room-by-room cleaning checklist, and advice on scent and air quality considerations to create a pleasant environment for prospective buyers.

In Chapter 7, we'll discuss how to showcase your home's best features. You'll learn how to identify your home's unique selling points and highlight key features in each room. Plus, we'll provide tips for capturing your home's essence through high-quality photography.

Pricing your home competitively is crucial for attracting offers. Chapter 8 will help you understand local market trends, the role of a comparative market analysis, and how to work with a real estate agent to determine the right price for your home.

Preparing for an open house is the focus of Chapter 9. You'll learn how to schedule and promote your open house, set up and host the event, and collect feedback and follow up with potential buyers.

Chapter 10 will guide you through navigating offers and negotiations. We'll cover reviewing and evaluating offers, counteroffers and negotiating strategies, and what to expect when accepting an offer and moving forward.

Finally, in Chapter 11, we'll discuss preparing for closing. You'll find tips for completing final repairs and updates, packing and moving strategies, and an overview of the closing process.

Throughout "Selling Made Simple: A Comprehensive Guide to Preparing Your House for Sale," we aim to provide you with the tools and knowledge you need to feel confident and in control during the home-selling process. By following the advice in this book, you'll be well-equipped to create a home that stands out from the competition and appeals to a wide range of potential buyers.

As you read through each chapter, remember that every home and situation is unique. While the principles outlined in this book apply to most home sales, it's essential to consider your specific circumstances and adjust the strategies as needed. You may choose to work closely with a real estate agent or other professionals to help you navigate the process and tailor the advice to your home and local market conditions.

In the Conclusion, we'll celebrate your successful home sale and offer some tips for settling into your new home. We'll also provide resources for further reading and support, ensuring you have everything you need to move forward with confidence.

The journey of selling your home can be both exciting and challenging, but with the right guidance, it doesn't have to be overwhelming. We hope that "Selling Made Simple: A Comprehensive Guide to Preparing Your House for Sale" serves as a valuable resource to help you prepare your home for the market and achieve a successful, stress-free sale.

By taking the time to read this book and implement the strategies discussed, you are already well on your way to making your home sale a rewarding experience. So, let's embark on this journey together, as we work step-by-step to prepare your house for sale and set the stage for a successful transaction. Happy selling!

Chapter 1: The Importance of Preparing Your House for Sale

Preparing your house for sale is a crucial step in the home-selling process. A well-prepared home can attract more potential buyers, receive higher offers, and sell more quickly. In this chapter, we will discuss the importance of preparing your house for sale and provide you with practical tips and insights to help you achieve the best possible outcome.

The Competitive Market

In today's competitive real estate market, it's essential to make your house stand out among the competition. Buyers have numerous options, and they're looking for a home that not only meets their needs but also feels warm, welcoming, and move-in ready. By taking the time to prepare your house for sale, you're creating an environment that appeals to a wide range of buyers, making it more likely that your home will sell quickly and for top dollar.

First Impressions Matter

When potential buyers arrive at your home, they will form an immediate impression based on the exterior appearance and overall atmosphere. A well-maintained, inviting exterior and a clean, organized interior can make a world of difference in a buyer's perception of your home. By investing time and effort in preparing your house for sale, you're ensuring that buyers see your home in its best light, which can ultimately lead to a more favorable impression and a higher likelihood of receiving offers.

Highlighting Your Home's Unique Features

Every home has its unique features and selling points, and it's essential to showcase them effectively when preparing your house for sale. By emphasizing your home's strengths and addressing any weaknesses, you're making it easier for potential buyers to visualize themselves living in the space and appreciate the value it offers. This can lead to increased interest, more showings, and, ultimately, a successful sale.

Reducing Time on Market

Homes that are well-prepared for sale tend to spend less time on the market. When your house is clean, organized, and in good repair, buyers are more likely to make an offer quickly, reducing the amount of time your home sits on the market. This not only minimizes the stress associated with selling a home, but it can also save you money on carrying costs like mortgage payments, utilities, and maintenance.

Increasing the Final Sale Price

Preparing your house for sale can have a direct impact on the final sale price. By addressing necessary repairs and updates, decluttering, and staging your home, you're creating an environment that appeals to a wide range of buyers. This can lead to increased competition and potentially multiple offers, ultimately driving up the sale price. In fact, according to the National Association of Realtors, staged homes sell for an average of 6% to 10% more than non-staged homes.

Building Buyer Confidence

Buyers want to feel confident that they're making a wise investment when purchasing a home. By presenting a well-maintained, move-in ready home, you're assuring potential buyers that your house has been well cared for and is a sound investment. This can lead to a smoother sales process, as buyers are less likely to request extensive repairs or renegotiate the sale price during the inspection period.

The Emotional Aspect

Selling a home can be an emotional experience, as you're saying goodbye to a space filled with memories and embarking on a new chapter in your life. By taking the time to prepare your house for sale, you're also preparing yourself emotionally for the transition. This can make the process feel less overwhelming and help you come to terms with the change.

Seven Practical Steps for Preparing Your House for Sale

Now that we've discussed the importance of preparing your house for sale, let's explore some practical steps you can take to ensure your home is in its best possible condition:

1. Assess your home's condition: Walk through your home and make a list of necessary repairs and updates. Prioritize these items based on their impact on your home's appearance and functionality. Consider consulting with a professional home inspector to identify any hidden issues that could arise during the buyer's inspection.

2. Declutter and organize: Remove excess items from your home to create a spacious, inviting atmosphere. This includes clearing out closets, cabinets, and storage areas. Organize your remaining belongings to demonstrate the functionality and storage potential of your home.

3. Deep clean: Ensure your home is spotless from top to bottom. Pay special attention to high-traffic areas, kitchens, and bathrooms, as these spaces can significantly influence a buyer's perception of your home. Consider hiring a professional cleaning service to achieve a thorough, deep clean.

4. Make necessary repairs and updates: Address the items on your repair and update list, focusing on those that will have the most significant impact on your home's appearance and value. This may include fixing leaky faucets, replacing outdated fixtures, or repainting walls in neutral colors.

5. Stage your home: Arrange furniture, lighting, and décor to create a welcoming, visually appealing environment. Highlight your home's best features and minimize any weaknesses. Consider hiring a professional stager if you're unsure how to stage your home effectively.

6. Boost curb appeal: Enhance your home's exterior appearance by maintaining your lawn, landscaping, and entryway. Make necessary repairs, repaint your front door, and add attractive outdoor lighting to create a warm, welcoming first impression.

7. Price your home competitively: Research local market trends and work with a real estate agent to determine the right price for your home. An appropriately priced home will attract more potential buyers and increase the likelihood of receiving multiple offers.

By following these practical steps, you'll be well on your way to preparing your house for sale and reaping the benefits of your hard work and dedication. Keep in mind that each home and situation is unique, so tailor these steps to best suit your specific circumstances.

In conclusion, the importance of preparing your house for sale cannot be overstated. A well-prepared home can attract more potential buyers, receive higher offers, and sell more quickly. By investing time and effort into presenting your home in its best light, you're setting the stage for a successful, rewarding home sale experience. With the tips and insights provided in this chapter, you'll be well-equipped to navigate the home-selling process with confidence and achieve the best possible outcome for your sale.

Notes: _____

_____

_____

_____

The home-selling process overview

Understanding the home-selling process is essential to achieving a successful sale. This chapter will provide an overview of the key steps involved in selling your home, from the initial preparation and listing to the final closing. By gaining a clear understanding of the process, you can better prepare your home and navigate the sale with confidence.

Step 1: Assessing Your Home's Condition

Before listing your home, it's essential to assess its condition and identify any necessary repairs and updates. Walk through your home and make a list of items that need attention, such as peeling paint, outdated fixtures, or damaged flooring. Prioritize these tasks based on their impact on your home's appearance and value. Addressing these issues before listing will help ensure your home is in its best possible condition and appeals to a wide range of buyers.

Step 2: Preparing Your Home for Sale

Once you've assessed your home's condition, it's time to prepare it for the market. This involves decluttering, deep cleaning, and staging your home to create an inviting, visually appealing environment. Enhance your home's curb appeal by attending to the exterior appearance, landscaping, and entryway. The better your home looks and feels, the more likely it is to attract potential buyers and receive higher offers.

Step 3: Pricing Your Home

Determining the right price for your home is a critical step in the selling process. Research local market trends and work with a real estate agent to conduct a comparative market analysis (CMA). A CMA will help you understand the value of similar homes in your area and determine a competitive price for your property. Pricing your home accurately will increase the likelihood of attracting offers and achieving a successful sale.

Step 4: Listing and Marketing Your Home

Once your home is prepared and priced appropriately, it's time to list and market your property. Work with a real estate agent to create a compelling listing description and high-quality photos that showcase your home's best features. Your agent will help you list your home on the Multiple Listing Service (MLS) and promote it through various marketing channels, such as online platforms, social media, and open houses.

Step 5: Showings and Open Houses

As potential buyers express interest in your home, you'll need to accommodate showings and possibly host open houses. Keep your home clean and organized during this period to create a positive impression on buyers. Be prepared to be flexible with showing times, as accommodating buyers' schedules can increase the likelihood of receiving offers.

Step 6: Reviewing and Negotiating Offers

Once you start receiving offers, you'll need to review and evaluate them carefully. Work with your real estate agent to assess each offer's terms and conditions, including the proposed sale price, contingencies, and closing timeline. You may need to negotiate with potential buyers to reach an agreement that meets your needs and preferences. This can involve making counteroffers and engaging in a back-and-forth dialogue until both parties are satisfied.

Step 7: Completing Due Diligence

After accepting an offer, the buyer will typically conduct a home inspection to ensure there are no hidden issues with your property. Be prepared to address any concerns that arise during this process, as unresolved issues can delay or jeopardize the sale. The buyer may also request additional contingencies, such as securing financing or selling their current home before closing on your property.

Step 8: Closing the Sale

Once all contingencies have been met, it's time to close the sale. The closing process involves signing various documents, transferring the title of your property to the buyer, and paying any required fees, such as agent commissions and closing costs. Your real estate agent will guide you through this process and ensure all paperwork is completed accurately and on time.

Step 9: Moving Out and Handing Over the Keys

Once the sale is complete, you'll need to move out of your home and hand over the keys to the new owners. This involves packing up your belongings, hiring a moving company or renting a truck, and ensuring your home is clean and in good condition for the new owners. Be sure to transfer utilities and cancel any services associated with your property, such as lawn care or pest control.

Step 10: Celebrating Your Successful Home Sale

After closing the sale and moving out, it's time to celebrate your successful home sale and begin the next chapter of your life. Reflect on the lessons learned throughout the process and use this experience to inform your future real estate decisions. Whether you're moving into a new home, downsizing, or relocating, take the time to enjoy the accomplishment of selling your home and moving forward.

Conclusion

The home-selling process can be complex and challenging, but with a clear understanding of the key steps involved, you can navigate the sale with confidence and achieve a successful outcome. By assessing your home's condition, preparing it for sale, pricing it accurately, and working closely with a real estate agent, you can ensure your home appeals to potential buyers and receives competitive offers.

Throughout this process, it's essential to remain flexible, patient, and focused on your ultimate goal: selling your home for the best possible price and terms. By following the steps outlined in this chapter and utilizing the resources and strategies provided throughout this book, you'll be well-equipped to navigate the home-selling process and achieve a successful, rewarding sale.

Notes: _____

_____

_____

_____

Organization Tips for Maintaining a Tidy Home During Showings

Maintaining a clean and organized home during the showing process is crucial to making a great impression on potential buyers. While it can be challenging to keep your home tidy and clutter-free, especially if you're still living in it, adopting some simple organization tips and daily habits can help you maintain an inviting atmosphere throughout the home-selling process.

In this section, we will provide a checklist of organization tips to help you effortlessly maintain a tidy home during showings.

Checklist for Maintaining a Tidy Home:

1. Create a daily routine: Establish a routine that includes daily tasks to keep your home clean and organized. This may involve making the beds, doing the dishes, wiping down surfaces, and picking up clutter. By sticking to this routine, you can ensure your home is always ready for showings.

2. Use storage solutions: Invest in storage solutions, such as bins, baskets, and drawer organizers, to help keep your belongings organized and out of sight. By having designated storage spaces for frequently used items, you can quickly tidy up before showings and maintain a clutter-free environment.

3. Have a designated "staging area": Set up a designated area in your home, such as a closet or storage room, to store items that need to be hidden away during showings. This can include personal items, paperwork, or laundry. By having a dedicated staging area, you can easily declutter your living spaces without scrambling to find temporary storage solutions.

4. Keep a cleaning caddy handy: Create a cleaning caddy filled with essential cleaning supplies, such as multi-surface cleaner, glass cleaner, microfiber cloths, and paper towels. Keep this caddy easily accessible so you can quickly address any spills or messes before showings.

5. Minimize personal items: As much as possible, minimize the number of personal items on display in your home. By keeping your belongings to a minimum, you can create a more neutral and inviting environment for potential buyers.

6. Regularly declutter: Set aside time each week to declutter and reorganize your living spaces. This can help you stay on top of any clutter that accumulates and ensures your home remains tidy and organized throughout the selling process.

7. Create a checklist for showings: Develop a checklist of tasks to complete before each showing. This may include tasks such as turning on lights, opening curtains or blinds, setting the thermostat to a comfortable temperature, and doing a final walk-through to ensure all clutter and personal items are out of sight.

8. Enlist family members' help: If you have family members living with you, encourage them to participate in maintaining a clean and organized home. Assign specific tasks to each family member and create a shared sense of responsibility for keeping the home ready for showings.

9. Make it easy to clean up: Keep a hamper in each bedroom and a wastebasket in every room to make it easy for you and your family members to quickly clean up any clutter or trash.

10. Stay prepared for last-minute showings: While it's essential to maintain a tidy home throughout the selling process, it's especially important to be prepared for last-minute showings. By following these organization tips and maintaining a daily routine, you can feel confident that your home will always be ready to impress potential buyers.

By incorporating these organization tips and strategies into your daily routine, you can ensure that your home remains clean, organized, and inviting throughout the showing process. By maintaining a clutter-free and welcoming environment, you can make a lasting impression on potential buyers and increase your chances of a successful sale.

Notes: _____

_____

_____

_____

Chapter 2: Assessing Your Home's Condition

Introduction

Before listing your home for sale, it's crucial to assess its condition and identify any areas that need improvement. By addressing necessary repairs and updates, you can ensure your home appeals to a wide range of buyers and maximizes its potential value. In this chapter, we'll guide you through the process of assessing your home's condition, identifying potential issues, and prioritizing repairs and updates.

Step 1: Conduct a Thorough Walkthrough

Begin by conducting a thorough walkthrough of your home, both inside and outside. Take note of any visible damage, wear and tear, or outdated features that could negatively impact a potential buyer's perception of your home. Pay special attention to high-traffic areas, such as the kitchen and bathrooms, as these spaces tend to experience more wear and tear and can significantly influence a buyer's decision.

Step 2: Make a List of Repairs and Updates

As you conduct your walkthrough, make a list of repairs and updates that may be necessary. This list may include items such as:

- Fixing leaky faucets or plumbing issues
- Repairing or replacing damaged flooring
- Updating outdated fixtures and hardware
- Addressing any electrical issues
- Painting walls in neutral colors
- Repairing or replacing damaged doors and windows
- Addressing any structural or foundation concerns

Remember that every home is unique, and the specific repairs and updates needed will vary depending on the age, style, and condition of your property.

Notes: _____

_____

_____

_____

Step 3: Prioritize Repairs and Updates

Once you've compiled a list of necessary repairs and updates, prioritize these tasks based on their impact on your home's appearance and value. Focus on items that will have the most significant effect on potential buyers, such as functional issues, safety concerns, and cosmetic improvements that enhance your home's overall appeal.

Some high-priority repairs and updates may include:

- Addressing structural or foundation issues
- Repairing or replacing damaged or leaking roofs
- Fixing major plumbing or electrical problems
- Updating outdated or non-functioning appliances
- Replacing severely worn or damaged flooring
- Painting walls in neutral colors

Step 4: Consult with a Professional Home Inspector

To ensure you've identified all potential issues with your home, consider consulting with a professional home inspector. An inspector can provide a comprehensive evaluation of your home's condition and identify any hidden problems that could arise during the buyer's inspection. By addressing these issues proactively, you can avoid unexpected surprises and costly delays during the sale process.

Step 5: Consider the Local Market Conditions

When assessing your home's condition and determining which repairs and updates to prioritize, it's essential to consider the local market conditions. In a seller's market, where demand for homes is high, and inventory is low, you may not need to make as many updates to attract buyers. However, in a buyer's market, where there is more competition among sellers, making improvements to your home can help it stand out and command a higher price.

Step 6: Set a Budget and Timeline

Finally, establish a budget and timeline for addressing necessary repairs and updates. Be realistic about what you can afford to invest in your home, and remember that not all improvements will yield a significant return on investment. Consult with a real estate agent or contractor to help you determine the most cost-effective updates and prioritize your spending accordingly.

Conclusion

Assessing your home's condition is a vital step in the home-selling process. By taking the time to identify necessary repairs and updates, you can ensure your home is in its best possible condition and appeals to a wide range of buyers. Additionally, by addressing potential issues proactively, you can avoid unexpected surprises and costly delays during the sale process.

Notes: _____

_____

_____

_____

Identifying Necessary Repairs and Updates

A well-maintained home is more likely to attract potential buyers and command a higher sale price. To make your home as appealing as possible, it's essential to identify and address necessary repairs and updates.

In this chapter, we'll discuss how to pinpoint which repairs and updates your home may need, and how to prioritize them to maximize your return on investment.

Step 1: Focus on Functionality and Safety

When identifying necessary repairs and updates, start by focusing on issues that affect the functionality and safety of your home. These issues may include:

- Plumbing problems, such as leaky faucets or pipes
- Electrical issues, including outdated wiring or faulty outlets
- Structural concerns, such as foundation cracks or sagging floors
- Roof damage or leaks
- Heating, ventilation, and air conditioning (HVAC) system issues

Addressing these functional and safety concerns should be your top priority, as they can significantly impact a buyer's perception of your home and its overall value.

Step 2: Evaluate Cosmetic Improvements

After addressing functional and safety concerns, turn your attention to cosmetic improvements that can enhance your home's appeal. These updates can make your home feel more modern, fresh, and inviting to potential buyers. Some common cosmetic updates include:

- Painting walls in neutral colors
- Replacing outdated light fixtures
- Updating hardware, such as door handles and cabinet pulls
- Repairing or replacing damaged or worn flooring
- Refreshing bathroom fixtures, such as faucets and showerheads
- Installing new kitchen appliances

Keep in mind that cosmetic updates should complement the style and character of your home. Aim for a cohesive, updated look that will appeal to a wide range of buyers.

Step 3: Consider Energy Efficiency Upgrades

Energy-efficient homes are increasingly in demand among today's buyers, who are looking for ways to reduce their environmental impact and save on utility costs. Consider upgrading to energy-efficient appliances, installing a programmable thermostat, or adding insulation to improve your home's energy efficiency. These updates can be a selling point and help set your home apart from the competition.

Step 4: Enhance Curb Appeal

The exterior of your home is the first impression potential buyers will have, so it's essential to make it as appealing as possible. Some repairs and updates that can enhance your home's curb appeal include:

- Painting or updating your home's siding
- Repairing or replacing damaged gutters and downspouts
- Maintaining your lawn and landscaping
- Updating outdoor lighting fixtures
- Repairing or replacing damaged walkways and driveways
- Adding new house numbers or a fresh coat of paint to your front door

Step 5: Prioritize Your Repairs and Updates

Once you've identified necessary repairs and updates, prioritize them based on their potential impact on your home's value and appeal. Focus on high-impact projects that will provide the most significant return on investment, such as functional and safety improvements, cosmetic updates, and energy-efficient upgrades.

Step 6: Consult with a Real Estate Professional

A real estate professional can provide valuable guidance on which repairs and updates are most likely to yield a high return on investment in your local market. They can also help you determine the best way to allocate your budget and ensure your home stands out among the competition.

Consult with a professional: the benefits of a pre-sale home inspection

Consulting with a professional for a pre-sale home inspection offers numerous benefits for homeowners preparing to sell their property. A thorough inspection can identify potential issues that may otherwise go unnoticed, providing valuable insights into the condition of your home and helping you make informed decisions about necessary repairs and updates.

In this chapter, we'll explore the advantages of a pre-sale home inspection and how it can contribute to a smoother, more successful home-selling process.

First and foremost, a pre-sale home inspection provides an objective evaluation of your home's condition, giving you a clear understanding of any underlying issues that may need to be addressed before listing your property. By identifying these problems early on, you can proactively address them and avoid any unexpected surprises or delays during the buyer's inspection or closing process. This proactive approach can also help you avoid potential negotiations or concessions that may arise if a buyer discovers an issue during their inspection.

In addition to uncovering hidden problems, a pre-sale home inspection can also help you prioritize repairs and updates that will have the most significant impact on your home's appeal and value. The inspector's report can serve as a valuable guide for determining which improvements are essential and which are less critical. This information can help you allocate your budget more effectively and ensure that you invest in the most impactful updates to enhance your property's desirability.

Another benefit of a pre-sale home inspection is that it can serve as a powerful marketing tool when listing your home. By sharing the inspection report with potential buyers, you can demonstrate transparency and instill confidence in the condition of your property. This openness can make your home more attractive to buyers and may even result in a quicker sale, as they will have a better understanding of what to expect when purchasing your home.

A pre-sale home inspection can also help you accurately price your property. By having a clear understanding of your home's condition and any necessary repairs, you can factor these costs into your asking price, ensuring that it accurately reflects the value of your home. This information can also help you negotiate with buyers more effectively, as you will have a solid understanding of the costs associated with any repairs or updates they may request.

Finally, a pre-sale home inspection can provide peace of mind for both you and the buyer. By addressing any issues upfront, you can feel confident in the condition of your home and its readiness for sale. For the buyer, the inspection report serves as reassurance that they are making a sound investment, ultimately contributing to a smoother, more successful transaction for both parties.

Consulting with a professional for a pre-sale home inspection offers numerous benefits for homeowners preparing to sell their property. By providing valuable insights into your home's condition, helping you prioritize repairs and updates, serving as a powerful marketing tool, and contributing to accurate pricing and smoother negotiations, a pre-sale home inspection can significantly enhance your home-selling experience. By investing in this essential step, you can ensure that you are well-prepared for the challenges of the real estate market and well-equipped to achieve a successful sale.

Notes: _____

_____

_____

_____

Chapter 4: Decluttering and Organizing - Creating an Inviting Space for Buyers

Introduction

When preparing your home for sale, one of the most critical steps is decluttering and organizing your living spaces. By creating a clean, clutter-free environment, you can showcase your home's true potential and make it more inviting to potential buyers. A well-organized and decluttered home not only appears larger and more spacious, but it also allows buyers to envision themselves living in the space more easily.

In this chapter, we will discuss the importance of decluttering and organizing your home, along with practical tips and strategies to help you create an appealing and welcoming atmosphere for prospective buyers.

Decluttering and organizing your home can have a significant impact on its appeal and perceived value. A cluttered, disorganized space can be off-putting to potential buyers, making it difficult for them to see past your personal belongings and imagine themselves living in the property. By removing excess items and organizing your living spaces, you can create a more visually appealing environment that allows buyers to focus on your home's best features.

The process of decluttering and organizing begins with evaluating each room in your home, identifying items that can be removed or stored away, and creating a plan for organizing and tidying up the remaining items.

This process may seem daunting at first, but by breaking it down into manageable tasks and focusing on one room at a time, you can systematically declutter and organize your entire home.

Notes: _____

_____

_____

_____

As you begin the decluttering process, consider the following tips and strategies to help you create an inviting, clutter-free space:

1. Adopt a minimalist approach: Remove as many personal items and decorations as possible, leaving only essential furniture and a few carefully chosen decorative pieces. This minimalist approach can make your home feel more spacious and allows potential buyers to imagine their own belongings in the space.

2. Depersonalize your space: Remove family photos, personal memorabilia, and other items that showcase your personal tastes and preferences. This depersonalization helps buyers see your home as a blank canvas, making it easier for them to envision themselves living there.

3. Organize closets and storage spaces: Buyers will likely inspect closets, cabinets, and other storage spaces, so it's essential to ensure these areas are tidy and well-organized. Remove any unnecessary items and consider using storage solutions, such as bins or baskets, to keep these spaces neat and clutter-free.

4. Clean and declutter surfaces: Clear countertops, tables, and other surfaces of clutter, leaving only essential items or a few carefully chosen decorative pieces. This clean, uncluttered look can make your home feel more spacious and welcoming.

5. Use storage solutions to your advantage: Invest in storage solutions, such as shelves, bins, or drawer organizers, to help you keep your home organized and clutter-free. These solutions can make it easier for you to maintain a tidy, inviting environment throughout the home-selling process.

Decluttering and organizing your home is a critical step in preparing your property for sale. By creating a clean, clutter-free environment, you can showcase your home's true potential and make it more appealing to potential buyers.

With a well-organized and decluttered home, you can enhance your property's overall appeal, helping you attract more prospective buyers and ultimately achieve a successful sale.

The Psychology of Decluttering and Room-by-Room Decluttering Strategies

Decluttering is not just about creating a visually appealing space; it also has significant psychological benefits for both the homeowner and potential buyers. Understanding the psychology behind decluttering can help you approach the process more effectively and better appreciate its importance in preparing your home for sale.

Furthermore, by implementing room-by-room decluttering strategies, you can create an environment that appeals to buyers on both a conscious and subconscious level, ultimately increasing the likelihood of a successful sale.

The psychology of decluttering is rooted in the idea that our physical environment can have a profound impact on our mental and emotional well-being. Cluttered spaces can create feelings of stress, anxiety, and overwhelm, making it difficult for individuals to focus and feel at ease.

On the other hand, decluttered and organized spaces can foster a sense of calm, order, and control. When potential buyers enter a decluttered home, they are more likely to experience positive emotions and develop a favorable impression of the property.

Additionally, decluttering can help to depersonalize a space, allowing buyers to more easily envision themselves living in the home. When a home is filled with personal belongings, family photos, and other items that reflect the current owner's tastes and preferences, it can be challenging for buyers to imagine their own lives in the space.

By decluttering and depersonalizing, you create a neutral environment that invites buyers to project their own dreams and aspirations onto the property.

Notes: _____

_____

_____

_____

To effectively declutter your home, it's essential to develop a systematic approach that addresses each room individually. By focusing on one room at a time, you can break the decluttering process into manageable tasks that will ultimately result in a cohesive, inviting home. The following room-by-room decluttering strategies can help guide your efforts:

1. Living Room: In the living room, focus on creating a comfortable and welcoming atmosphere. Remove excess furniture and decorative items, leaving only essential pieces that contribute to the room's function and aesthetic. Organize and store away items like books, magazines, and remote controls to create clean, uncluttered surfaces. If you have built-in shelves, consider displaying a curated selection of items to showcase the room's storage potential without overwhelming the space.

2. Kitchen: The kitchen is often considered the heart of the home, so it's essential to create an organized and functional space. Clear countertops of appliances and other items, leaving only a few essential tools or decorative pieces. Organize cabinets and drawers, removing any unnecessary items or duplicates. If you have a pantry, ensure that it's tidy and well-organized, showcasing the room's storage capabilities.

3. Bedrooms: In the bedrooms, focus on creating a serene and restful environment. Remove personal items and decorations, opting for neutral bedding and simple wall decor. Organize closets and dressers, ensuring that they appear spacious and functional. Remove any clutter from nightstands and other surfaces, leaving only a few essential items, such as a lamp and an alarm clock.

4. Bathrooms: In the bathrooms, aim for a clean and spa-like atmosphere. Remove personal toiletries and cleaning products, storing them out of sight. Display only a few carefully chosen items, such as a decorative soap dispenser or a potted plant. Organize cabinets and drawers, ensuring that they are tidy and free of clutter. Replace old towels and bathmats with fresh, neutral-colored options.

5. Home Office: If you have a home office, focus on creating an organized and productive space. Clear surfaces of papers, files, and office supplies, storing them neatly in drawers or filing cabinets. Organize bookshelves and remove any personal items or distractions. Ensure that the workspace is clean, functional, and conducive to productivity, as this will appeal to buyers who may need a dedicated area for work or study.

6. Garage and Outdoor Spaces: Don't forget about the garage and outdoor living spaces when decluttering your home. In the garage, organize tools, equipment, and stored items, creating a clean and functional space that showcases its storage and workspace potential. In outdoor living areas, such as patios and decks, remove any clutter or extraneous items and arrange furniture to create a welcoming and inviting atmosphere. Maintain landscaping, and ensure that walkways and driveways are clean and well-maintained.

By implementing these room-by-room decluttering strategies, you can create a cohesive, inviting, and appealing environment that will resonate with potential buyers on a psychological level. The process of decluttering not only enhances the visual appeal of your home but also fosters a sense of calm and order that buyers will appreciate.

Furthermore, by depersonalizing the space and creating a neutral environment, you encourage buyers to envision their own lives and aspirations in the property, ultimately increasing the likelihood of a successful sale.

In conclusion, understanding the psychology of decluttering and implementing targeted room-by-room strategies can significantly improve the overall appeal of your home and contribute to a more successful home-selling process.

By creating a clean, organized, and inviting environment, you tap into potential buyers' emotions and desires, making it easier for them to imagine themselves living in your property. As a result, your home will stand out in the competitive real estate market, increasing your chances of attracting the right buyer and achieving a successful sale.

Organization Tips for Maintaining a Tidy Home During Showings

Maintaining a clean and organized home during the showing process is crucial to making a great impression on potential buyers. While it can be challenging to keep your home tidy and clutter-free, especially if you're still living in it, adopting some simple organization tips and daily habits can help you maintain an inviting atmosphere throughout the home-selling process.

In this section, we will provide a checklist of organization tips to help you effortlessly maintain a tidy home during showings.

Checklist for Maintaining a Tidy Home:

1. Create a daily routine: Establish a routine that includes daily tasks to keep your home clean and organized. This may involve making the beds, doing the dishes, wiping down surfaces, and picking up clutter. By sticking to this routine, you can ensure your home is always ready for showings.

2. Use storage solutions: Invest in storage solutions, such as bins, baskets, and drawer organizers, to help keep your belongings organized and out of sight. By having designated storage spaces for frequently used items, you can quickly tidy up before showings and maintain a clutter-free environment.

3. Have a designated "staging area": Set up a designated area in your home, such as a closet or storage room, to store items that need to be hidden away during showings. This can include personal items, paperwork, or laundry. By having a dedicated staging area, you can easily declutter your living spaces without scrambling to find temporary storage solutions.

4. Keep a cleaning caddy handy: Create a cleaning caddy filled with essential cleaning supplies, such as multi-surface cleaner, glass cleaner, microfiber cloths, and paper towels. Keep this caddy easily accessible so you can quickly address any spills or messes before showings.

5. Minimize personal items: As much as possible, minimize the number of personal items on display in your home. By keeping your belongings to a minimum, you can create a more neutral and inviting environment for potential buyers.

6. Regularly declutter: Set aside time each week to declutter and reorganize your living spaces. This can help you stay on top of any clutter that accumulates and ensures your home remains tidy and organized throughout the selling process.

7. Create a checklist for showings: Develop a checklist of tasks to complete before each showing. This may include tasks such as turning on lights, opening curtains or blinds, setting the thermostat to a comfortable temperature, and doing a final walk-through to ensure all clutter and personal items are out of sight.

8. Enlist family members' help: If you have family members living with you, encourage them to participate in maintaining a clean and organized home. Assign specific tasks to each family member and create a shared sense of responsibility for keeping the home ready for showings.

9. Make it easy to clean up: Keep a hamper in each bedroom and a wastebasket in every room to make it easy for you and your family members to quickly clean up any clutter or trash.

10. Stay prepared for last-minute showings: While it's essential to maintain a tidy home throughout the selling process, it's especially important to be prepared for last-minute showings. By following these organization tips and maintaining a daily routine, you can feel confident that your home will always be ready to impress potential buyers.

By incorporating these organization tips and strategies into your daily routine, you can ensure that your home remains clean, organized, and inviting throughout the showing process. By maintaining a clutter-free and welcoming environment, you can make a lasting impression on potential buyers and increase your chances of a successful sale.

Notes: _____

_____

_____

_____

Chapter 4: Staging Your Home for Success - Creating an Irresistible First Impression

Introduction

Once you have decluttered, organized, and addressed any necessary repairs and updates, the next step in preparing your home for sale is staging. Staging is the art of arranging your home's interior and exterior spaces in a way that showcases its best features and creates an inviting atmosphere for potential buyers.

A well-staged home can make a powerful first impression, drawing buyers in and helping them envision themselves living in the space. In this chapter, we will explore the importance of staging your home for success, and provide practical tips and strategies to help you create a visually appealing and emotionally resonant environment that will set your home apart in the competitive real estate market.

Staging your home is not just about creating an aesthetically pleasing space; it's also about tapping into the emotions and desires of potential buyers. When buyers walk into a well-staged home, they are more likely to experience positive emotions, such as comfort, warmth, and a sense of belonging.

These feelings can be powerful motivators in the home-buying process, often prompting buyers to make an offer or choose one home over another. Moreover, a professionally staged home can help your property stand out in online listings, attracting more prospective buyers and potentially resulting in a quicker sale at a higher price.

The process of staging your home involves strategically arranging furniture, decor, and lighting to accentuate your home's best features and create a welcoming atmosphere.

Notes: _____

_____

_____

_____

While some homeowners choose to hire professional stagers, it is possible to achieve stunning results on your own with a bit of creativity, effort, and attention to detail. To help guide your staging efforts, consider the following key principles:

1. Create a focal point: In each room, identify a feature that you'd like to highlight, such as a fireplace, a large window, or an architectural detail. Arrange furniture and decor to draw attention to this focal point, making it the center of interest in the room.

2. Use neutral colors: When choosing paint colors, bedding, and other textiles, opt for neutral tones that will appeal to a wide range of buyers. Neutral colors can create a calming, inviting atmosphere and allow potential buyers to envision their own belongings in the space.

3. Showcase functionality: Arrange furniture in a way that showcases the room's purpose and makes the space feel functional and inviting. For example, in the living room, create a comfortable seating area around a coffee table or focal point, and ensure there is adequate lighting for reading or conversation.

4. Opt for minimal decor: When accessorizing your home, choose a few carefully selected pieces that add visual interest without overwhelming the space. Consider using items that reflect the local culture or natural environment, as this can help create a sense of connection to the community.

5. Pay attention to lighting: Lighting plays a crucial role in creating a welcoming atmosphere and showcasing your home's best features. Ensure that each room has a mix of ambient, task, and accent lighting, and consider using dimmer switches to create a warm, inviting glow.

Staging your home for success is an essential step in the home-selling process that can help you create a powerful first impression and attract more potential buyers. By understanding the principles of staging and implementing practical strategies, you can transform your home into an inviting, visually appealing space that resonates with buyers on both an emotional and aesthetic level.

In the following sections of this chapter, we will delve deeper into specific staging tips and techniques for various areas of your home, helping you create a cohesive and irresistible presentation that sets your property apart in the competitive real estate market.

Staging Basics

Effective home staging involves carefully considering furniture arrangement, lighting, and color schemes to create an inviting atmosphere that appeals to potential buyers.

Whether you choose to stage your home yourself or hire a professional stager, understanding the basic principles and techniques of staging can help you achieve the desired results.

Checklist for Furniture Arrangement, Lighting, and Color Schemes

Checklist for Staging Basics:

1. Furniture Arrangement:
   o Create a focal point in each room, and arrange furniture to highlight this feature.
   o Use appropriately sized furniture that doesn't overwhelm the space.
   o Arrange furniture in a way that showcases the room's functionality and purpose.
   o Ensure there is a clear path for foot traffic and avoid blocking doorways or windows.
   o Consider using furniture with clean lines and neutral colors that appeal to a wide range of buyers.

2. Lighting:
   o Use a mix of ambient, task, and accent lighting to create a welcoming atmosphere in each room.
   o Maximize natural light by opening curtains and blinds, and ensure windows are clean.
   o Consider using dimmer switches to create a warm, inviting glow.
   o Replace any burnt-out light bulbs and ensure all light fixtures are clean and functioning properly.
   o Use floor lamps, table lamps, and wall sconces to add layers of light and highlight architectural features.

3. Color Schemes:
   o Choose neutral paint colors that appeal to a wide range of buyers and create a calm, inviting atmosphere.
   o Use coordinating colors for textiles, such as bedding, window treatments, and throw pillows.
   o Avoid overly bold or personal color choices that may not resonate with all buyers.
   o Consider using accent colors sparingly to add visual interest without overwhelming the space.

4. DIY Staging vs. Hiring a Professional Stager:
   o Assess your budget, time constraints, and personal abilities when deciding whether to stage your home yourself or hire a professional stager.
   o Consider the potential return on investment of professional staging, as it may lead to a quicker sale and higher sale price.
   o Keep in mind that professional stagers have access to a wide range of furniture, decor, and resources that can help create a polished, cohesive look.
   o If you choose to stage your home yourself, be prepared to invest time and effort in decluttering, cleaning, and arranging your space.
   o Seek inspiration from home staging resources, such as books, magazines, and websites, to help guide your DIY staging efforts.

Notes: _____

_____

_____

_____

DIY Staging vs. Hiring a Professional Stager

Both DIY staging and hiring a professional stager have their advantages and drawbacks. The choice ultimately depends on your budget, time constraints, and personal abilities.

DIY staging can be a cost-effective option for homeowners who are willing to invest time and effort into preparing their home for sale. By decluttering, cleaning, and carefully arranging furniture, lighting, and decor, you can create an inviting atmosphere that appeals to potential buyers. However, DIY staging can be time-consuming, and it may not achieve the same level of polish and sophistication as professional staging.

Hiring a professional stager, on the other hand, can provide a more polished and cohesive look, as these professionals have access to a wide range of furniture, decor, and resources. Additionally, professional stagers have experience in creating visually appealing spaces that resonate with buyers, which may lead to a quicker sale and higher sale price. However, hiring a professional stager can be expensive, and the cost may not always be justified by the potential return on investment.

Notes: _____

_____

_____

_____

Chapter 5: Curb Appeal - Making a Great First Impression

The exterior of your home is the first thing potential buyers see, and it plays a crucial role in shaping their initial impressions of your property. A well-maintained and visually appealing exterior, known as curb appeal, can attract more prospective buyers, make your home stand out in the competitive real estate market, and ultimately contribute to a successful sale.

In this chapter, we will delve into the importance of curb appeal and provide practical tips and strategies for enhancing your home's exterior, creating a lasting positive impression that entices buyers to explore the property further.

From landscaping to exterior maintenance and lighting, we will guide you through the process of transforming your home's facade into a welcoming and appealing showcase that captures the attention and imagination of potential buyers.

Landscaping and Lawn Care, Exterior Maintenance and Repairs, and Enhancing Your Entryway: Door, Lighting, and Hardware

A well-maintained and visually appealing exterior can significantly impact a potential buyer's perception of your home. In this paragraph, we will provide a checklist of essential tasks and strategies for improving your home's curb appeal, focusing on landscaping and lawn care, exterior maintenance and repairs, and enhancing your entryway.

Notes: _____

_____

_____

_____

Checklist for Curb Appeal:

Landscaping and Lawn Care:

- o Keep your lawn mowed, edged, and free of weeds.
- o Water your lawn regularly to maintain a healthy, green appearance.
- o Prune trees and shrubs to keep them looking neat and well-maintained.
- o Remove any dead or dying plants and replace them with healthy, attractive specimens.
- o Add colorful, seasonal flowers and plants to create visual interest and enhance your home's overall appeal.
- o Apply fresh mulch to garden beds to create a clean, polished look.
- o Keep walkways and driveways clean, free of debris, and in good repair.

Exterior Maintenance and Repairs:

- o Inspect your home's exterior for signs of wear, damage, or deterioration, such as peeling paint, cracked siding, or loose shingles.
- o Address any necessary repairs promptly, as these issues can detract from your home's overall appearance and may raise concerns for potential buyers.
- o Clean your home's exterior, including siding, windows, and gutters, to remove dirt, grime, and debris.
- o Power wash your driveway, walkways, and patio to create a clean and well-maintained appearance.
- o Repaint or re-stain your home's exterior, if necessary, to refresh its appearance and protect it from the elements.

Enhancing Your Entryway:

- o Update your front door by repainting or refinishing it, or consider replacing it with a new, more visually appealing door.
- o Clean and polish door hardware, such as knobs, locks, and hinges, or replace outdated hardware with new, modern options.
- o Install attractive, well-functioning outdoor lighting to illuminate your entryway, ensuring it is welcoming and safe for visitors.
- o Add a new doormat, potted plants, or other decorative elements to create a warm and inviting atmosphere.
- o Ensure your house number is clearly visible and easy to read from the street.

By addressing these key aspects of your home's exterior, you can create a lasting first impression that entices potential buyers to explore your property further.

As you work on improving your home's curb appeal, remember that the goal is to create a cohesive, visually appealing presentation that resonates with buyers on both an emotional and aesthetic level. This may involve investing in new plants, paint, or hardware, as well as dedicating time to regular maintenance and upkeep. However, the potential return on investment, in terms of a quicker sale and a higher sale price, can make these efforts well worth it in the long run.

Notes: _____

_____

_____

_____

Chapter 6: Deep Cleaning - Preparing Your Home for Showings

Introduction

In addition to decluttering, organizing, and staging your home, deep cleaning is a crucial step in preparing your property for showings and open houses. A spotlessly clean home not only enhances its visual appeal, but also signals to potential buyers that the property has been well-maintained and cared for.

In this chapter, we will guide you through the process of deep cleaning your home, ensuring every nook and cranny is immaculate and ready to impress even the most discerning buyer. From tackling high-traffic areas to addressing often-overlooked details, we will provide practical tips and strategies for creating a pristine environment that highlights your home's best features and makes it stand out in the competitive real estate market.

By investing time and effort into thoroughly cleaning your home, you can create a lasting positive impression that increases the likelihood of a successful sale and helps you achieve the best possible return on your investment.

General Cleaning Tips and Tricks

A thorough deep cleaning of your home is essential for creating a lasting impression on potential buyers. In this paragraph, we will provide a checklist of general cleaning tips and tricks to help you achieve a spotless and well-maintained home that appeals to a wide range of buyers.

Checklist for General Cleaning Tips and Tricks:

1. Create a cleaning plan:
   - List all the rooms and areas in your home that need cleaning.
   - Prioritize tasks based on their importance and the time they will take to complete.
   - Break down larger tasks into smaller, more manageable steps.

2. Gather the necessary supplies:
   - Stock up on cleaning supplies, such as all-purpose cleaners, glass cleaner, disinfectants, and microfiber cloths.
   - Ensure you have specialized cleaning products for specific surfaces or materials, such as wood polish, tile cleaner, or stainless steel cleaner.
   - Keep your cleaning supplies organized and easily accessible.

o

3. Start from the top and work your way down:
   o Begin by dusting high surfaces, such as ceiling fans, light fixtures, and crown molding.
   o Progress to lower surfaces, such as shelves, countertops, and furniture.
   o Finish by vacuuming or sweeping floors, ensuring all dust and debris have been removed.

4. Pay attention to often-overlooked areas:
   o Clean baseboards, window sills, and door frames.
   o Wipe down light switches, outlet covers, and door handles.
   o Remove cobwebs from corners, both inside and outside your home.

5. Use the right tools and techniques:
   o Use microfiber cloths for effective dusting and cleaning without leaving lint behind.
   o Utilize vacuum cleaner attachments to reach tight spaces and corners.
   o Employ appropriate cleaning techniques for specific surfaces, such as using a soft cloth for delicate materials or a scrub brush for more durable surfaces.

6. Focus on high-traffic areas:
   o Deep clean carpets, especially in hallways and living areas, using a carpet cleaner or professional service.
   o Scrub and mop hard-surface floors, paying extra attention to high-traffic zones.
   o Clean and disinfect frequently-touched surfaces, such as countertops, door handles, and light switches.

7. Don't forget the exterior:
   o Power wash siding, walkways, and driveways.
   o Clean windows, both inside and out.
   o Sweep porches, patios, and decks to remove debris and cobwebs.

By following this checklist of general cleaning tips and tricks, you can ensure your home is spotlessly clean and ready to impress potential buyers. A well-maintained and immaculate home not only enhances its visual appeal but also signals to buyers that the property has been well-cared-for, increasing the likelihood of a successful sale.

Room-by-Room Cleaning Checklist

A systematic, room-by-room approach to cleaning can help ensure that no area of your home is overlooked, creating a consistently clean and well-maintained environment that appeals to potential buyers. In this paragraph, we will provide a room-by-room cleaning checklist to guide you through the deep cleaning process and help you achieve the best possible results.

Checklist for Room-by-Room Cleaning:

1. Entryway:
   o Sweep or vacuum the floors.
   o Wipe down walls, baseboards, and door frames.
   o Clean light fixtures, switches, and outlet covers.
   o Polish door hardware and clean windows.
   o Dust any furniture or decorative items.

2. Living Room:
   o Vacuum carpets and upholstery, including beneath cushions.
   o Dust all surfaces, including shelves, tables, and electronics.
   o Wipe down walls, baseboards, and door frames.
   o Clean light fixtures, switches, and outlet covers.
   o Wash windows and clean window treatments.

3. Kitchen:
   o Clean and disinfect countertops, sinks, and faucets.
   o Wipe down cabinets, handles, and drawer pulls.
   o Clean appliances, including the oven, refrigerator, and microwave.
   o Wash walls, baseboards, and door frames.
   o Sweep and mop the floors.
   o Empty and clean the trash can.

4. Dining Room:
   o Dust all surfaces, including the table, chairs, and any display items.
   o Clean light fixtures, switches, and outlet covers.
   o Wipe down walls, baseboards, and door frames.
   o Vacuum or sweep and mop the floors.

5. Bedrooms:
   o Vacuum carpets and clean hard-surface floors.
   o Dust all surfaces, including furniture, shelves, and electronics.
   o Wipe down walls, baseboards, and door frames.
   o Clean light fixtures, switches, and outlet covers.
   o Wash windows and clean window treatments.
   o Launder bedding and make beds.

6. Bathrooms:
   o Scrub and disinfect toilets, bathtubs, and showers.
   o Clean and disinfect sinks, countertops, and faucets.
   o Wipe down mirrors, cabinets, and shelves.
   o Wash walls, baseboards, and door frames.
   o Sweep and mop the floors.
   o Replace towels and bathmats with clean, fresh linens.

7. Laundry Room:
   o Wipe down the washer and dryer, including lint traps and control panels.
   o Clean countertops, sinks, and faucets.
   o Sweep and mop the floors.
   o Wash walls, baseboards, and door frames.

8. Garage:
   o Sweep or vacuum the floors.
   o Wipe down walls, baseboards, and door frames.
   o Dust and organize shelves and storage areas.
   o Clean garage door hardware and windows.

By following this room-by-room cleaning checklist, you can ensure that every area of your home is thoroughly cleaned and ready for showings. In addition to the detailed cleaning tasks listed above, it's essential to consider scent and air quality when preparing your home for sale.

Notes: _____

_____

_____

_____

Scent and Air Quality Considerations:

- Air out your home by opening windows and doors, allowing fresh air to circulate and eliminate any lingering odors.
- Clean or replace air filters in your HVAC system to improve air quality and remove dust and allergens.
- Avoid using strong, artificial air fresheners, as they may be off-putting to some buyers. Instead, opt for subtle, natural scents, such as essential oil diffusers or potpourri.
- Address any potential sources of unpleasant odors, such as pet bedding, garbage cans, or damp areas.

Consider baking cookies or simmer ing a pot of water with cinnamon sticks and citrus peels to create a pleasant, welcoming aroma during showings.

Taking these scent and air quality considerations into account can create a comfortable, inviting atmosphere for potential buyers, further enhancing your home's appeal. By implementing the room-by-room cleaning checklist and addressing scent and air quality concerns, you can ensure that your home is well-prepared for showings and creates a lasting positive impression on potential buyers.

In conclusion, a thorough deep cleaning of your home, following a room-by-room checklist, is essential for creating a consistently clean and well-maintained environment that appeals to potential buyers. Additionally, paying attention to scent and air quality can further enhance the overall atmosphere, making your home more inviting and increasing the likelihood of a successful sale. By investing time and effort into preparing your home for showings, you can create a lasting impression that helps you achieve the best possible return on your investment in the competitive real estate market.

Notes: _____

_____

_____

_____

Chapter 7: Identifying Your Home's Unique Selling Points

Introduction

When preparing your home for sale, it is essential to identify its unique selling points, the features and characteristics that make it stand out in the crowded real estate market.

By highlighting these key attributes, you can create a lasting impression on potential buyers and increase the likelihood of a successful sale. In this chapter, we will guide you through the process of identifying your home's unique selling points, helping you showcase its most appealing qualities and maximize its potential value.

Checklist for Identifying Your Home's Unique Selling Points:

1. Analyze your home's architecture and design:
    o Take note of any distinctive architectural features, such as archways, exposed brick walls, or high ceilings.
    o Consider the overall design style of your home, such as modern, traditional, or transitional.
    o Identify any unique design elements, such as custom cabinetry, built-in bookcases, or a fireplace.

2. Assess your home's functionality and layout:
    o Consider the flow of your home, taking note of any open spaces or well-defined rooms.
    o Take note of any functional spaces that are highly desirable, such as a home office, a media room, or a mudroom.
    o Identify any special features, such as a gourmet kitchen, a master suite, or a large backyard.

3. Evaluate your home's location and surroundings:
    o Consider the convenience and accessibility of your location, such as proximity to schools, shopping, or public transportation.
    o Take note of any desirable neighborhood amenities, such as parks, trails, or community centers.
    o Identify any scenic or natural surroundings, such as a waterfront view or a wooded lot.

4. Consider recent updates and renovations:
   - Take note of any recent updates or renovations that have added value to your home, such as a new roof, HVAC system, or kitchen appliances.
   - Consider any renovations that have improved your home's livability, such as a finished basement or updated bathrooms.
   - Identify any energy-efficient upgrades, such as new windows, insulation, or solar panels.

5. Seek input from a real estate professional:
   - Consult with a real estate agent or appraiser to gain an outside perspective on your home's unique selling points.
   - Ask for feedback on the features that are most likely to appeal to potential buyers in your local market.
   - Consider any recommended updates or improvements that could enhance your home's value and appeal.

By following this checklist for identifying your home's unique selling points, you can gain a deeper understanding of what makes your property stand out and appeal to potential buyers.

Once you have identified your home's unique features and characteristics, you can leverage them in your marketing materials, staging, and showing strategies, helping to create a lasting impression on potential buyers and increase the likelihood of a successful sale.

In addition to identifying your home's unique selling points, it is also essential to create a cohesive, visually appealing presentation that highlights these features and appeals to a broad range of buyers. This may involve updating your decor, rearranging furniture, or investing in professional staging services.

By taking a strategic and comprehensive approach to showcasing your home's best features, you can create a memorable experience for potential buyers and maximize your chances of a successful sale.

Notes: _____

_____

_____

_____

Highlighting Key Features in Each Room and The Power of Photography

Once you have identified your home's unique selling points, it's time to showcase them in each room of your home. In this paragraph, we will provide a checklist of tips for highlighting key features in each room and capturing your home's essence through photography.

Checklist for Highlighting Key Features in Each Room:

1. Define the purpose of each room:
   o Ensure that each room has a clear and defined purpose, whether it is a bedroom, living room, or home office.
   o Consider the potential needs and desires of potential buyers, and stage each room accordingly.

2. Highlight unique features:
   o Focus on the most attractive features of each room, such as a fireplace, bay window, or built-in bookcase.
   o Use lighting to accentuate these features and draw attention to them.

3. Use color and texture to create visual interest:
   o Consider the color palette of each room, and use complementary or contrasting colors to create visual interest.
   o Use textures and patterns to add depth and dimension to each space.

4. Eliminate clutter:
   o Remove any unnecessary items from each room to create a clean and organized space.
   o Keep surfaces clean and uncluttered to showcase the potential of each room.

Notes: _____

_____

_____

_____

In addition to highlighting key features in each room, photography is a powerful tool for showcasing your home's unique characteristics and creating a positive first impression on potential buyers. Here are some tips for capturing your home's essence through photography:

1. Use natural light:
   o Photograph each room during the day, when natural light is at its best.
   o Open curtains and blinds to let in as much natural light as possible.

2. Stage each room:
   o Ensure each room is clean, uncluttered, and staged to showcase its potential.
   o Add decorative touches, such as fresh flowers or colorful pillows, to create an inviting atmosphere.

3. Capture the unique features:
   o Use close-up shots to highlight unique features, such as architectural details or custom finishes.
   o Consider using a wide-angle lens to capture the entire room and showcase its potential.

By following these tips for highlighting key features in each room and capturing your home's essence through photography, you can create a compelling visual presentation that draws potential buyers in and encourages them to explore your property further.

Remember that a picture is worth a thousand words, and investing in professional photography services can pay off in the form of increased buyer interest and a higher sale price.

Notes: _____

_____

_____

_____

Chapter 8: Pricing Your Home Competitively

Introduction

When it comes to selling your home, pricing is one of the most critical factors in determining its success on the market. Setting the right price can mean the difference between a quick, successful sale and a property that languishes on the market for months or even years.

In this chapter, we will explore strategies for pricing your home competitively, helping you strike the right balance between maximizing your return on investment and appealing to potential buyers.

Pricing your home competitively requires a combination of market research, analysis, and strategy. By taking a data-driven approach and considering factors such as comparable properties, local market trends, and economic indicators, you can arrive at a price point that accurately reflects the value of your home and attracts potential buyers.

In addition, pricing your home competitively can help you avoid the pitfalls of overpricing or underpricing, both of which can lead to missed opportunities and decreased interest from potential buyers.

In the following sections, we will explore the key factors that contribute to a successful pricing strategy, such as understanding the local market, setting realistic expectations, and working with a real estate professional. By following these guidelines and taking a thoughtful, strategic approach to pricing your home, you can increase your chances of a successful sale and achieve the best possible return on your investment.

Notes: _____

_____

_____

_____

Understanding Local Market Trends

When it comes to pricing your home competitively, it's crucial to have a deep understanding of the local real estate market and the trends that are shaping it. This knowledge can help you make informed decisions about pricing and position your home effectively in the market. Here are some tips for understanding local market trends:

Checklist for Understanding Local Market Trends:

1. Research comparable properties:
   - Look at recently sold properties in your area that are similar in size, style, and condition to your home.
   - Consider the asking price and final sale price of these properties to get a sense of market demand and price expectations.

2. Analyze market data:
   - Look at key market indicators, such as the average days on market, the number of homes for sale, and the median sale price in your area.
   - Consider how these trends are evolving over time and how they may impact your pricing strategy.

3. Consider the broader economic climate:
   - Look at factors such as job growth, population trends, and interest rates to get a sense of the broader economic climate in your area.
   - Consider how these factors may impact the demand for housing and your pricing strategy.

4. Work with a real estate professional:
   - Consult with a real estate agent who has experience in your local market and can provide you with insights and analysis based on their expertise.
   - Consider their recommendations for pricing and positioning your home in the market.

By understanding local market trends, you can set a realistic price that reflects the current demand for housing in your area and appeals to potential buyers. This can increase the likelihood of a successful sale and help you achieve the best possible return on your investment.

Resources to better understand local market trends

Here is a checklist of resources and sources that homeowners can follow to better understand local market trends:

1. Real estate websites:
   - Websites such as Zillow, Redfin, and Realtor.com provide data on local market trends, including recent sales, average days on market, and inventory levels.

2. Local real estate associations:
   - Local real estate associations often provide market reports and analysis that can help homeowners understand current market trends.

3. Local newspapers and media outlets:
   - Newspapers and media outlets often publish real estate market reports that provide insights into local trends and conditions.

4. Real estate agents:
   - Real estate agents have access to up-to-date market data and can provide homeowners with insights and analysis based on their expertise.

5. Government sources:
   - Government sources such as the U.S. Census Bureau and the Bureau of Labor Statistics provide data on local economic conditions that can impact the housing market.

6. Local economic development organizations:
   - Economic development organizations often provide data and analysis on local economic conditions, including job growth, population trends, and industry trends.

7. Homeowner associations:
   - Homeowner associations can provide insights into local housing trends and conditions, as well as information on any upcoming developments or projects that may impact the housing market.

By using these resources and sources, homeowners can gain a better understanding of local market trends and make informed decisions about pricing and positioning their home in the market. This can help them achieve a successful sale and maximize their return on investment.

The Role of a Comparative Market Analysis and Working with a Real Estate Agent to Determine the Right Price

One of the most effective ways to determine the right price for your home is to work with a real estate agent who can provide you with a comparative market analysis (CMA).

A CMA is a report that compares your home to similar properties in your area that have recently sold or are currently on the market. By analyzing this data, your agent can help you arrive at a price that accurately reflects the value of your home and appeals to potential buyers.

Here are some checklists for understanding the role of a comparative market analysis and working with a real estate agent to determine the right price:

Checklist for the Role of a Comparative Market Analysis:

1. Analyzing comparable properties:
   o Your agent will analyze recently sold properties that are similar to yours in size, style, and condition to determine a price range for your home.
   o They will also consider currently active listings and how they compare to your home.

2. Reviewing market trends:
   o Your agent will review current market trends and economic indicators to determine the current demand for housing in your area.
   o They will also consider how these trends may impact the pricing of your home.

3. Adjusting for differences:
   o Your agent will adjust the price range based on any differences between your home and comparable properties, such as location, age, or amenities.

Notes: _____

_____

_____

_____

Checklist for Working with a Real Estate Agent to Determine the Right Price:

1. Choose an experienced agent:
   - Look for an agent with experience in your local market and a track record of successful sales.
   - Consider their knowledge of market trends, pricing strategies, and negotiation skills.

2. Discuss your goals and priorities:
   - Talk to your agent about your goals for selling your home, such as maximizing your return on investment or selling quickly.
   - Discuss your priorities and concerns, such as pricing, marketing, and showing strategies.

3. Review the comparative market analysis:
   - Carefully review the CMA provided by your agent, paying attention to the comparable properties used and the adjustments made.
   - Discuss any questions or concerns with your agent and consider their recommendations for pricing your home.

4. Monitor market conditions:
   - Keep an eye on local market trends and economic indicators, and discuss any changes with your agent.
   - Consider adjusting your price or marketing strategy if market conditions shift.

By working with a real estate agent and utilizing a comparative market analysis, you can arrive at a price for your home that accurately reflects its value and appeals to potential buyers. This can increase the likelihood of a successful sale and help you achieve the best possible return on your investment.

Notes: _____

_____

_____

_____

Chapter 9: Preparing for an Open House

Introduction

An open house is a crucial event in the home selling process, providing potential buyers with an opportunity to view your property, ask questions, and get a sense of whether it might be a good fit for their needs. Preparing for an open house requires careful planning and attention to detail, as it can have a significant impact on the success of your sale.

In this chapter, we will explore strategies for preparing your home for an open house, helping you create a welcoming and inviting atmosphere that draws potential buyers in and encourages them to envision themselves living in your space.

Preparing for an open house involves a range of tasks, from cleaning and organizing to staging and marketing. By taking a proactive approach and considering the needs and preferences of potential buyers, you can create a positive first impression that sets the stage for a successful sale.

In the following sections, we will explore tips and checklists for preparing your home for an open house, including everything from deep cleaning and decluttering to curb appeal and marketing strategies. By following these guidelines and taking a thoughtful, strategic approach to your open house, you can increase your chances of a successful sale and achieve the best possible return on your investment.

Notes: _____

_____

_____

_____

Scheduling and Promoting Your Open House

Scheduling and promoting your open house is a critical step in the home selling process, as it helps generate interest and attract potential buyers to your property. Here are some tips and a checklist for scheduling and promoting your open house:

Checklist for Scheduling and Promoting Your Open House:

1. Set a date and time:
    o Choose a date and time that is convenient for potential buyers, such as a weekend afternoon.
    o Consider scheduling your open house during a local event or festival to attract more visitors.

2. Advertise your open house:
    o Use social media platforms like Facebook and Instagram to advertise your open house.
    o List your open house on real estate websites and local event calendars.

3. Notify neighbors:
    o Inform your neighbors about your open house to increase visibility and potentially attract buyers who are interested in the neighborhood.
    o Consider inviting neighbors to your open house to create a welcoming and friendly atmosphere.

4. Prepare marketing materials:
    o Create flyers or brochures that highlight the key features of your home and provide information on the open house.
    o Place these materials in visible locations around your neighborhood and in local businesses.

By scheduling and promoting your open house effectively, you can generate interest and attract potential buyers to your property. Be sure to consider the needs and preferences of your target audience and use a range of marketing strategies to maximize visibility and exposure. Remember, the more people that attend your open house, the higher the chances of finding the right buyer for your home.

Open House Setup and Hosting Tips, Collecting Feedback, and Following Up with Potential Buyers

Hosting an open house can be a stressful and overwhelming experience, but with the right preparation and mindset, it can also be an opportunity to showcase your home and connect with potential buyers.

Here are some tips and a checklist for open house setup and hosting, as well as collecting feedback and following up with potential buyers:

Checklist for Open House Setup and Hosting:

1. Clean and declutter your home:
   o Ensure your home is clean and free of clutter, creating a welcoming and inviting atmosphere.
   o Consider hiring a professional cleaning service to deep clean your home before the open house.

2. Enhance curb appeal:
   o Make sure your lawn is mowed, landscaping is trimmed, and the exterior of your home is clean and well-maintained.
   o Consider adding fresh flowers or potted plants to enhance curb appeal.

3. Create a welcoming atmosphere:
   o Consider baking cookies or lighting candles to create a warm and inviting atmosphere.
   o Play soft background music to set the tone for a relaxing and enjoyable experience.

4. Be prepared to answer questions:
   o Be knowledgeable about the features of your home and ready to answer any questions that potential buyers may have.
   o Consider providing a list of upgrades or improvements that you have made to the home.

Notes: _____

_____

_____

_____

Checklist for Collecting Feedback and Following Up with Potential Buyers:

1. Provide feedback forms:
   - Provide potential buyers with feedback forms to fill out after viewing your home.
   - Ask for their honest feedback on the overall presentation, price, and any features they liked or disliked.

2. Follow up with potential buyers:
   - Follow up with potential buyers after the open house to answer any additional questions they may have.
   - Consider sending a thank you note or email to show your appreciation for their interest.

By setting up and hosting your open house effectively, you can create a positive and memorable experience for potential buyers, increasing the likelihood of a successful sale.

Collecting feedback and following up with potential buyers can also provide valuable insights into how your home is perceived and how you can make improvements to increase its appeal. Remember, a successful open house requires careful planning and attention to detail, but with the right approach, it can be a rewarding and enjoyable experience for both you and potential buyers.

Notes: _____

_____

_____

_____

Chapter 10: Navigating Offers and Negotiations

Introduction

After hosting an open house and generating interest in your home, you may begin to receive offers from potential buyers. Navigating the offer and negotiation process can be a complex and emotional experience, requiring careful consideration of the terms and conditions of each offer and effective communication with potential buyers.

In this chapter, we will explore strategies for navigating offers and negotiations, helping you understand the process and make informed decisions that support your goals and priorities.

Negotiating offers involves a range of factors, from the initial price offered to the terms of the sale, such as closing dates and contingencies. By understanding these factors and considering your priorities and preferences, you can make informed decisions that support your goals for selling your home.

In the following sections, we will explore tips and checklists for navigating offers and negotiations, including strategies for evaluating and comparing offers, effective communication with potential buyers, and finalizing the terms of the sale. By following these guidelines and taking a thoughtful, strategic approach to negotiations, you can achieve the best possible return on your investment and ensure a successful sale.

Notes: _____

_____

_____

_____

Reviewing and Evaluating Offers, Counteroffers and Negotiating Strategies, and Accepting an Offer and Moving Forward

Once you've hosted your open house and generated interest in your home, potential buyers may begin to make offers on your property. Reviewing and evaluating offers, counteroffers and negotiating strategies, and ultimately accepting an offer and moving forward can be a complex and emotional process. Here are some tips and checklists for each step in the process:

Reviewing and Evaluating Offers

Checklist for Reviewing and Evaluating Offers:

1. Review each offer carefully:
    o Consider the terms of the offer, such as the purchase price, closing date, and any contingencies or special conditions.
    o Evaluate each offer based on your priorities and goals for selling your home.

2. Compare offers:
    o Compare each offer side-by-side, looking at the overall financial terms as well as any contingencies or special conditions.
    o Consider the financial strength of the buyer, including their ability to secure financing.

3. Consider the risks:
    o Consider any potential risks associated with each offer, such as the possibility of the sale falling through due to financing or inspection issues.

4. Seek professional advice:
    o Consult with your real estate agent and attorney to ensure that you fully understand the terms and conditions of each offer.

Notes: _____

_____

_____

_____

Counteroffers and Negotiating Strategies

Checklist for Counteroffers and Negotiating Strategies:

1. Be clear about your priorities:
   - Be clear about your priorities and goals for selling your home, such as maximizing your return on investment or selling quickly.
   - Consider your priorities when making counteroffers or negotiating.

2. Evaluate the buyer's position:
   - Consider the buyer's position and ability to negotiate.
   - Evaluate their motivation to buy and their financial strength.

3. Consider multiple offers:
   - If you receive multiple offers, consider using them to negotiate a higher price or better terms.
   - Use the competition to your advantage.

4. Stay flexible:
   - Remain flexible throughout the negotiation process, and be willing to compromise on non-essential terms to reach an agreement.

Notes: _____

_____

_____

_____

Accepting an Offer and Moving Forward

Checklist for Accepting an Offer and Moving Forward:

1. Finalize the terms:
   - Finalize the terms of the sale with the buyer and ensure that both parties are in agreement.
   - Ensure that all necessary paperwork is completed and signed.

2. Prepare for closing:
   - Prepare for closing by gathering all necessary documents and ensuring that all necessary repairs or maintenance have been completed.
   - Work with your real estate agent and attorney to ensure that everything is in order.

3. Transfer ownership:
   - Transfer ownership of the property to the buyer, and ensure that all necessary documentation is filed with the appropriate authorities.

4. Celebrate your sale:
   - Celebrate your successful sale and the achievement of your goals.

By following these tips and checklists for reviewing and evaluating offers, counteroffers and negotiating strategies, and accepting an offer and moving forward, you can navigate the home selling process with confidence and achieve the best possible outcome.

Remember to stay focused on your priorities and work closely with your real estate agent and attorney to ensure that everything is in order. With the right approach, you can achieve a successful sale and move forward with your next adventure.

Notes: _____

_____

_____

_____

Chapter 11: Preparing for Closing

Introduction

After you've accepted an offer on your home, the final step in the home selling process is closing. Preparing for closing involves a range of tasks, from gathering necessary documentation to ensuring that all necessary repairs and maintenance have been completed.

In this chapter, we will explore strategies for preparing for closing, helping you understand the process and make informed decisions that support your goals and priorities.

Closing can be a complex and time-consuming process, requiring careful attention to detail and effective communication with all parties involved in the transaction. In the following sections, we will explore tips and checklists for preparing for closing, including strategies for gathering necessary documents, preparing for the final walkthrough, and understanding the closing costs and fees associated with the sale.

By following these guidelines and taking a thoughtful, strategic approach to closing, you can ensure a smooth and successful transition to your next adventure.

Notes: _____

_____

_____

_____

Completing Final Repairs and Updates, Packing and Moving Strategies, and the Closing Process: What to Expect

After you've accepted an offer on your home, the final step in the home selling process is closing. Preparing for closing involves a range of tasks, from completing final repairs and updates to packing and moving strategies, and understanding the closing process. Here are some tips and checklists for each step in the process:

Completing Final Repairs and Updates

Checklist for Completing Final Repairs and Updates:

1. Review your contract:
   - Review your contract to ensure that all necessary repairs and updates have been completed.
   - Ensure that you have documentation of all completed repairs and updates.

2. Hire a professional:
   - Consider hiring a professional inspector to ensure that all necessary repairs and updates have been completed to a high standard.
   - Consider hiring a cleaning service to ensure that your home is spotless for the final walkthrough.

3. Address any last-minute issues:
   - Address any last-minute issues that may arise, such as repairs or maintenance that were missed during the initial inspection.

4. Ensure that everything is in order:
   - Ensure that everything is in order before the final walkthrough and closing.

Notes: _____

_____

_____

_____

Packing and Moving Strategies

Checklist for Packing and Moving Strategies:

1. Declutter and organize:
   - Declutter and organize your belongings to make packing and moving easier.
   - Consider donating or selling any items that you no longer need or want.

2. Hire a professional moving company:
   - Consider hiring a professional moving company to assist with the packing and moving process.
   - Ensure that you research and choose a reputable and reliable company.

3. Label boxes:
   - Label boxes clearly and organize them by room to make unpacking easier.
   - Consider packing a box of essentials for your first night in your new home.

4. Notify utility companies and change your address:
   - Notify utility companies of your move and arrange for services to be transferred or canceled.
   - Change your address with the post office and any necessary organizations.

Notes: _____

_____

_____

_____

The Closing Process: What to Expect

Checklist for the Closing Process:

1. Review the settlement statement:
   - Review the settlement statement to ensure that all terms of the sale are in order.
   - Ensure that all costs and fees associated with the sale are accounted for.

2. Attend the final walkthrough:
   - Attend the final walkthrough to ensure that the property is in the same condition as when the offer was accepted.
   - Address any last-minute issues that may arise during the walkthrough.

3. Sign necessary paperwork:
   - Sign all necessary paperwork and ensure that all necessary documentation is in order.
   - Work closely with your real estate agent and attorney to ensure that everything is in order.

4. Transfer ownership and receive payment:
   - Transfer ownership of the property to the buyer and receive payment for the sale.
   - Ensure that all necessary documentation is filed with the appropriate authorities.

By following these tips and checklists for completing final repairs and updates, packing and moving strategies, and understanding the closing process, you can ensure a smooth and successful transition to your next adventure.

Remember to stay organized, communicate effectively with all parties involved in the transaction, and work closely with your real estate agent and attorney to ensure that everything is in order. With the right approach, you can achieve a successful sale and move forward with confidence.

Chapter 12: Conclusion

In this book, we have explored the essential steps for preparing your home for sale, from assessing your home's condition to completing final repairs and updates, packing and moving strategies, and understanding the closing process. Selling a home can be a complex and emotional process, but with the right approach, you can achieve a successful sale that supports your goals and priorities.

Remember to stay focused on your priorities and communicate effectively with potential buyers and all parties involved in the transaction. Work closely with your real estate agent and attorney to ensure that everything is in order, and stay organized throughout the process to minimize stress and ensure a smooth transition.

Selling a home is a significant life event, and it's essential to approach the process with care and attention to detail. By following the tips and checklists in this book, you can navigate the home selling process with confidence and achieve a successful sale that supports your next adventure. Best of luck in your home selling journey!

Checklist for Celebrating Your Successful Sale and Settling into Your New Home:

1. Celebrate your successful sale:
   - Take time to celebrate your successful sale and the achievement of your goals.
   - Consider hosting a housewarming party to show off your new home to family and friends.
2. Unpack and organize:
   - Unpack and organize your belongings in your new home.
   - Consider hiring a professional organizer to help you get settled.
3. Get to know your new community:
   - Get to know your new community by exploring local shops, restaurants, and events.
   - Consider joining local organizations or groups to meet new people.
4. Make necessary updates:
   - Make necessary updates to your new home, such as painting or installing new fixtures.
   - Prioritize updates based on your preferences and goals for your new space.

By following these tips and checklists for celebrating your successful sale and settling into your new home, you can transition smoothly and enjoyably to your new space. Remember to take time to celebrate your achievements and stay focused on your priorities and goals for your new home. With the right approach, you can make your new house feel like a home in no time.

Resource Section

45-Point Checklist for Staging a Home for Sale

Staging a home for sale involves creating an appealing and inviting environment that allows potential buyers to envision themselves living in the space. Here is a comprehensive checklist of 45 key elements to consider when staging a home for sale:

1. Curb appeal: Enhance the exterior of your home by adding fresh paint, updating hardware, and adding plants.
2. Front porch: Create an inviting entrance with a clean and organized front porch.
3. Entryway: Create a welcoming entryway with a clean, organized, and decluttered space.
4. Flooring: Ensure that all floors are clean, polished, and in good condition.
5. Walls: Apply a fresh coat of paint in neutral colors to create a clean and inviting environment.
6. Lighting: Ensure that all rooms are well-lit and utilize a mix of natural and artificial lighting.
7. Furniture: Arrange furniture in a way that maximizes space and creates an inviting flow.
8. Artwork and decor: Add tasteful artwork and decor that enhances the style and personality of the home.
9. Rugs: Use area rugs to add texture and color to rooms.
10. Window treatments: Add window treatments that provide privacy while allowing natural light to enter.
11. Mirrors: Use mirrors to create the illusion of space and enhance natural light.
12. Bedding: Use high-quality bedding to create a luxurious and inviting bedroom.
13. Pillows and throws: Add accent pillows and throws to create a cozy and inviting environment.
14. Closet organization: Ensure that all closets are organized and decluttered to showcase storage space.
15. Bathroom towels: Use high-quality towels in bathrooms to create a spa-like atmosphere.
16. Shower curtains: Use shower curtains to create a clean and inviting environment in bathrooms.
17. Kitchen organization: Organize kitchen cabinets and drawers to showcase storage space and create an inviting environment.
18. Countertops: Clear countertops of clutter to create a clean and organized environment.
19. Appliances: Ensure that all appliances are clean and in good working condition.
20. Dining room: Set the dining room table with high-quality dishes and table settings.
21. Living room: Use decorative pillows and throws to create a cozy and inviting environment in the living room.

22. Home office: Create an organized and inviting home office space.
23. Guest bedroom: Create an inviting and comfortable guest bedroom with high-quality bedding and decor.
24. Children's bedrooms: Use playful decor and bedding to create a fun and inviting space for children.
25. Laundry room: Create an organized and functional laundry room.
26. Garage: Organize and declutter the garage to showcase storage space.
27. Outdoor living space: Create an inviting and comfortable outdoor living space with furniture and decor.
28. Pets: Remove pets from the home during showings and ensure that all pet-related items are stored out of sight.
29. Scents: Use subtle scents to create a welcoming and inviting environment, such as freshly baked cookies or candles.
30. Clutter: Remove all unnecessary clutter from the home to create a clean and organized environment.
31. Personal items: Remove all personal items such as photos and memorabilia to allow potential buyers to envision themselves living in the space.
32. Plants: Use plants to add life and color to rooms.
33. Storage space: Showcase storage space throughout the home, such as closets and cabinets.
34. Maintenance: Ensure that all necessary maintenance and repairs are completed before showings.
35. Cleanliness: Ensure that the home is spotless and clean for showings.
36. Safety: Ensure that the home is safe and free from hazards.
37. Seasonal decor: Use seasonal decor to create a festive and inviting environment.
38. Temperature: Keep the temperature comfortable for potential buyers during showings.
39. Accessible spaces: Ensure that all spaces in the home are accessible and easy to navigate.
40. Home technology: Showcase any home technology features, such as a smart home system or home theater.
41. Storage solutions: Add storage solutions, such as shelves and organizers, to maximize space and showcase storage options.
42. Room purpose: Clearly define the purpose of each room in the home to help potential buyers envision themselves living in the space.
43. Accent walls: Use accent walls to add interest and style to rooms.
44. Neutral decor: Use neutral decor to appeal to a wide range of potential buyers.
45. Welcome home sign: Create a simple "Welcome Home" sign and place it in the entry to your home during Open Houses.

Notes: _____

_____

Staging Your Home During the Spring and Summer Months

Staging a home during the spring and summer months presents unique challenges due to warmer weather and the potential for outdoor activities. However, with the right strategies and techniques, you can create an inviting and appealing environment that appeals to potential buyers. Here are some tips to help you stage your home during the spring and summer months.

Emphasize Outdoor Living Spaces:

- Clean and declutter all outdoor living spaces such as patios, decks, and gardens to showcase their potential.
- Add comfortable seating such as outdoor furniture, pillows, and cushions.
- Use outdoor lighting to create an inviting atmosphere for evening showings.
- Add pops of color with potted plants and flowers.

Keep Cool and Comfortable:

- Ensure that the air conditioning system is in good working condition and set to a comfortable temperature for showings.
- Use light and airy fabrics such as linen and cotton for bedding and window treatments.
- Use ceiling fans to circulate air and create a cool and comfortable atmosphere.
- Use light and bright decor to create a fresh and inviting atmosphere.

Notes: _____

_____

_____

_____

Staging Your Home During the Fall and Winter Months

Staging a home during the fall and winter months presents unique challenges due to colder weather and potential weather hazards. However, with the right strategies and techniques, you can create an inviting and appealing environment that appeals to potential buyers. Here are some tips to help you stage your home during the fall and winter months.

Keep Outside Access Open:

- Clear all leaves, snow, and debris from driveways, walkways, and entryways to ensure safe and easy access.
- Use a doormat or rug to prevent tracking in dirt and moisture.
- Use outdoor lighting to highlight key features of your home and to ensure safe access during darker hours.
- Keep landscaping maintained and tidy by trimming bushes and shrubs.

Tips to Keep the Inside Warm and Clean:

- Ensure that the heating system is in good working condition and set to a comfortable temperature for showings.
- Use area rugs and throws to create a cozy and inviting atmosphere.
- Clean all windows to maximize natural light and showcase outdoor views.
- Use seasonal decor such as wreaths, garlands, and pumpkins to create a festive atmosphere.
- Keep floors and carpets clean and dry to prevent slips and falls.
- Use scents such as cinnamon and vanilla to create a warm and inviting atmosphere.

Here are 17 Free and Inexpensive Ways to Stage your Home During the Fall and Winter Months:

1. Keep driveway, pathways, patios, decks, and steps to your home free from snow and ice.
2. Add a winter wreath to your front door.
3. Add a welcome mat at your front door. Bonus: this will also help buyers from tracking in snow and dirt from outside!
4. Add greenery to outdoor pots.
5. Put outdoor lights on timers so buyers are never arriving in the dark. This also allows people driving by to see your home.
6. Turn your thermostat up a few degrees to ensure buyers are comfortable, even on the coldest days.
7. If you have a gas fireplace, light a fire. Buyers will love to walk in and see a warm, crackling fire!
8. If you have a non-working fireplace, get creative and place candles, greenery, or vases inside of it.
9. Add a throw to the back of your couch and a warm blanket or quilt at the foot of each bed.
10. Open curtains and blinds and turn on each light in your house.
11. Simmer a few cinnamon sticks on the stove to create an inviting winter fragrance.
12. Clean your windows from the inside and out. If you have plastic over your windows, remove it so buyers can see the views.
13. Set your dining room table for a festive winter gathering. Think holiday cookies or soup bowls and terrines.
14. Place greenery or flowers around your home.
15. Include photographs of your yard, garden, patio, or deck in the summer so buyers know what they can look forward to in warmer months.
16. Highlight your home's features that are especially useful in winter. Think of an attached garage, new furnace, or energy-efficient windows.
17. Go ahead and decorate for the holidays, just keep it simple. Stick to a few elegant items like a holiday wreath or white twinkling lights. Too many items and you'll risk your home looking cluttered.

Notes: _____

_____

_____

_____

Zoom Town USA – The Next Step

If you are considering selling your home and looking for a new lifestyle, then the Zoom Town USA book is must-read. It provides a comprehensive guide to the remote work-life balance lifestyle and helps readers understand the steps needed to create a more meaningful and balanced lifestyle.

By reading the Zoom Town USA book, you will gain insight into what it means to live in a modern-rural community with the ability to work remotely, while also enjoying the beauty of nature and a slower paced lifestyle. This book can help you make the decision to move to a modern-rural area or simply create your own Zoom Town Lifestyle, which is all about being able to enjoy the amenities of modern living while living in harmony with nature.

The Zoom Town USA book provides readers with guidance on how to leave the stress and crime of the big city behind and embrace a more meaningful and balanced lifestyle. By understanding the Zoom Town Lifestyle and what it has to offer, you can make informed decisions about your future and create a life that is truly fulfilling.

In summary, if you are looking to sell your home and create a new lifestyle, then the Zoom Town USA book is must-read. It provides a comprehensive guide to the remote work-life balance lifestyle and helps readers understand the steps needed to create a more meaningful and balanced lifestyle.

Notes: _____

_____

_____

_____

_____

_____

_____

_____

_____

_____

_____

_____

_____

_____

Notes: _____

_____

_____

_____

_____

_____

_____

_____

_____

_____

_____

_____

_____

_____

_____

Notes: _____

_____

_____

_____

_____

_____

_____

_____

_____

_____

_____

_____

_____

_____

_____

Notes: _____

_____

_____

_____

_____

_____

_____

_____

_____

_____

_____

_____

_____

_____

_____

Notes: _____

_____

_____

_____

_____

_____

_____

_____

_____

_____

_____

_____

_____

_____

_____

Made in the USA
Columbia, SC
23 January 2024

30867893R00043